FOR KIDS BY A

Written by Benaiah S. Faagau

DEDICATION

This book is dedicated to all the children who are having a hard time with their parents getting a divorce. I hope it will help and encourage you during this very difficult time.

TABLE OF CONTENTS

INTRODUCTION

Since you've picked up this book, I'm guessing that you nee
help with understanding why your parents are getting a divorce
or maybe you feel like your emotions are out of control. If so,
wrote this book for you.

Life can be miserable when you first hear that your parents are getting a divorce. It may feel like the two people you love most in the world don't love you anymore. This isn't true. They just don't love each other anymore.

The worst part about divorce may be watching your parents slowly drift apart day after day until they go their separate ways. or maybe the divorce has come as a complete surprise to you. Whatever situation you find yourself in, the news is devastating.

In all the confusion and chaos, you might think the situation will only lead to destruction and brokenness. It's okay to tell your

THE BEGINNING

Is there someone in your life who you don't like being around? Maybe that person has hurt you in the past, or maybe they do things that annoy you. That might be how your parents feel around each other.

Do you ever find yourself asking why your mom and dad are fighting all the time? The thing is, parents get mad at each other for lots of different reasons. It could simply be because they can't agree on something. The next thing you know, one of them might be packing up their things.

BLAMING THE OTHER PERSON

Sometimes your parents might blame each other for absolutely everything. It might even feel like they're always looking for something to blame each other for.

Have you ever asked your parents to help you understand why they are getting a divorce? Then when you talk to them about it, do they say it is the other parent's fault? This is something no kid wants to hear.

MIXED EMOTIONS

You may feel overwhelmed by lots of different feelings. When my parents divorced, I felt sadness and grief. Once I was up all night crying because I didn't want my dad to leave after visiting me. It left me feeling empty inside.

Do you feel jealous of other kids who have parents who aren't fighting? Maybe you're angry because you see your parents hurting each other and only thinking about themselves. You might also feel abandoned, like your mom or dad left because they didn't want you.

At times, I also felt betrayed because I knew that this wasn't supposed to happen. My mom and dad were supposed to stay together forever. I learned the hard way that things don't always go as planned. This felt very unfair.

No matter how you feel, it is important to remember that there is always a good reason for your feelings and that they are completely normal.

IT'S NOT YOUR FAULT

Your parents' divorce is not your fault. Blaming yourself for their problems might feel like the easiest thing to do. Please understand that the divorce did not happen because of you, but because of your mom and dad's issues.

Even if your mom or dad leaves the house, it has NOTHING to do with you. Absolutely nothing. It is because of their adult problems.

YOU ARE NOT ALONE

One very important thing to remember is that you are not alone. It may feel like you are the only kid whose parents are going through a divorce, but that is not true. All around the world, lots of other kids' parents decide to divorce. Knowing that I was not alone in my parents' divorce gave me the courage to get through it and the desire to grow through it.

I also learned that it is tough to work through a divorce when you don't have anybody supporting you. Talking to people you trust about the divorce is a good way to process all of your emotions.

Who do you feel safe enough to talk to about your situation? This might be a close family friend, a grandparent or other relative, a counselor, a coach, a pastor, a teacher, or any other adult you trust.

Please do not try to work through this by yourself. I speak from experience.

FINGERS CROSSED

You may feel like your fingers are crossed every single day, hoping that your parents will come back together. This is very normal.

I felt this way when my parents divorced. I didn't want to live with one parent and never know when or if I would see the other one ever again. I never knew what would happen next.

You may feel panicked and ask, "What's happening to me?" Please know that it is easy for anxiety to take over your thoughts.

WHEN ANXIETY TAKES OVER

When my parents divorced, I felt anxious most days. I kept trying to think of ways I could fix things in our family so that everything would be perfect. I couldn't think of any. Then I realized that it wasn't my job to heal the problems between my parents.

Something that helps me when I feel anxious is to take a deep breath in and hold it for a few seconds. Then I slowly let my breath out. I do this until I am more relaxed and in control. Then I can think more clearly.

When I feel worried, I talk to God because I know He will always listen to me. He loves me and cares about my family and what we are going through.

Other things that might help you to feel calm are to pet your dog or to write about how you feel. It might also help to focus on something else, such as reading a book, listening to music, or doing something active that you enjoy—like going on a bike ride

BROKEN TRUST

Maybe one or both of your parents have broken your trust. Don't feel guilty if you find yourself in this situation.

My dad broke my trust when my parents divorced, but he is consistently working hard to earn it back. Hopefully, with time and patience, your parents will earn your trust back too.

LOSING FOCUS

When people go through a divorce, they often lose focus of what is important. It is like they see everything through blurred eyes. They might forget that family is what is really important: not food, not video games, and not even money.

Sometimes it can be hard to understand your parents when they act as if you don't exist. I remember feeling ignored and overlooked by my mom and dad when they were going through their divorce. These feelings hurt, and they can be overwhelming. They might even make you lose your focus, just like your parents have lost theirs.

If you feel like your emotions are too much for you to handle, the best thing to do is tell someone you trust. Let them know that you are overwhelmed and that you need their help and support.

LESSONS LEARNED

I have learned so much through my experience. If I could do things over again, I would ask my grandparents for their support. I also learned that no matter what my emotions were, they were normal. I didn't need to be ashamed of them.

Now that I'm older, I realize that my parents' divorce was not my fault. They chose this because they weren't happy anymore, not because of something I did or didn't do. Even though things didn't go as I wanted, I was able to work through my sadness and eventually have a healthy relationship with both parents. Even though my mom and dad are divorced now, I see that they both still love me very much.

If you are anything like me, you might feel overwhelmed and confused about all that is going on right now. As someone who has been through my own parent's divorce, I want to encourage you. You will get through this! The question is, how will you choose to grow through it?

ACKNOWLEDGMENTS

First, I would like to thank my dad for giving me the idea for this book. I want to thank both my mom and my dad for their encouragement and for walking with me through the process of writing it.

Taylor, Kavika, Kole, Dominic, Max, and Charese, I am so thankful to have you for my brothers and sisters.

Thanks to the launch team for all your help and support. I appreciate you so much.

ABOUT THE AUTHOR

Benaiah S. Faagau is a twelve-year-old boy who lives in Spokane, Washington. Some of his hobbies include board games, reading, and metal detecting. Benaiah also enjoys learning about stocks. A fun fact about Benaiah is that he likes playing football as a wide receiver.

Author, Benaiah S. Faagau

REVIEW ASK

Thank you for buying my book. It really means a lot to me. I want to grow as an author, so every honest review is priceless.

Please head over to Amazon (or wherever you bought this book) to leave a review. Thank you for your time. Have a great day!

Made in the USA
Coppell, TX
22 January 2022

72098152R00019